# Mediterranean Fish Stew

## INGREDIENTS

### Serves 4–6

4 tbsp olive oil

1 onion, peeled and finely sliced

5 garlic cloves, peeled and finely
sliced

1 fennel bulb, trimmed and finely
chopped

3 celery sticks, trimmed and finely
chopped

400 g can chopped tomatoes with
Italian herbs

1 tbsp freshly chopped oregano

1 bay leaf

rind and juice of 1 orange

1 tsp saffron strands

750 ml/11¼ pints fish stock

3 tbsp dry vermouth

salt and freshly ground
black pepper

225 g/8 oz thick haddock fillets

225 g/8 oz sea bass or bream fillets

225 g/8 oz raw tiger prawns, peeled

crusty bread, to serve

## TASTY TIP

When making a dish with as much
canned tomato as this, it is worth
buying a good-quality variety.

1 Heat the olive oil in a large saucepan. Add the onion, garlic, fennel and celery and cook over a low heat for 15 minutes, stirring frequently until the vegetables are soft and just beginning to turn brown.

2 Add the canned tomatoes with their juice, oregano, bay leaf, orange zest and juice with the saffron strands. Bring to the boil, then reduce the heat and simmer for 5 minutes. Add the fish stock and vermouth and season to taste with salt and pepper, then pour into the cooking dish. Cover with the lid and switch to high and cook for 1 hour.

3 Wipe or rinse the haddock and bass fillets and remove as many of the bones as possible. Place on a chopping board and cut into 5 cm/2 inch cubes. Add to the cooking dish and switch to auto. Cook for 30 minutes before adding the prawns and continue to cook for a further 20 minutes or until the prawns are cooked and have turned pink. Adjust the seasoning to taste and serve with crusty bread.

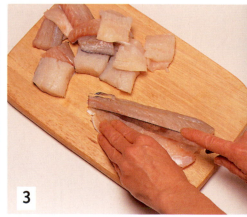

# Step-by-Step, Practical Recipes Slow Cooker: Contents

## Fish & Seafood Recipes

*Slow-cooked dishes are full of tender, flavoursome morsels, none more so than the delicious fish dishes listed below.*

## Meat Recipes

*Certain meats work really well in a slow cooker. The cooking time softens the meat so that it melts in the mouth!*

## Chicken Recipes

*Chicken will never be boring from a slow-cooker. The flavours of the seasonings and spices will really get to work, marinading the meat to perfection!*

## Vegetable Recipes

*Some vegetables dishes are made to be cooked in a slow cooker, especially if they also contain pulses.*

**48 Tips & Hints for the Slow Cooker**

FLAME TREE has been creating family-friendly, classic and beginner recipes for our bestselling cookbooks for over 12 years now. Our mission is to offer you a wide range of expert-tested dishes, while providing clear images of the final dish so that you can match it to your own results. We hope you enjoy this super selection of recipes – there are plenty more to try! Titles in this series include:

**Cupcakes • Slow Cooker • Curries Chinese • Soups • Baking Breads Cakes • Simple Suppers • Pasta Chicken • Fish & Seafood • Chocolate**

For more information please visit:
*www.flametreepublishing.com*

# Smoked Haddock Kedgeree

## INGREDIENTS

### Serves 4

50 g/2 oz butter
450 g/1 lb smoked haddock fillets
1 onion, peeled and finely chopped
2 tsp mild curry powder
175 g/6 oz easy-cook long-grain rice
450 ml/³⁄₄ pint fish or vegetable
  stock, heated
2 large eggs, hard-boiled and shelled
2 tbsp freshly chopped parsley
2 tbsp whipping cream (optional)
salt and freshly ground black pepper
pinch of cayenne pepper

## FOOD FACTS

Kedgeree is a simple, fulfilling dish originating from India. Flaked white fish, parsley, hard-boiled eggs and curry powder are combined with butter or cream for a delicious, tasty dish. Early Indian recipes also contained lentils.

1 Use a little of the butter to lightly grease the cooking dish. Place the haddock in the dish and pour in 300 ml/1/2 pint water. Cover with the lid and switch the cooker to high. Cook for 30 minutes or until tender.

2 Take the fish out and place on a board. Remove all the skin and bones from the fish and flake into a dish. Reserve.

3 Meanwhile, melt the remaining butter in a saucepan and add the chopped onion and curry powder. Cook, stirring, for 3–4 minutes, or until the onion is soft, then stir in the rice. Cook for a further minute, stirring continuously, then stir in the hot stock.

4 Transfer to the cleaned cooking dish and switch to high. Cover with the lid and cook for 40 minutes or until the rice is almost tender. Add the fish and continue to cook for a further 40 minutes or until the rice has absorbed all the liquid. Cut the eggs into quarters or eighths and add half to the mixture with half the parsley. Carefully stir in the cream, if using. Season to taste with salt and pepper. Heat the kedgeree for a further 15 minutes or until piping hot.

5 Transfer the mixture to a large dish and garnish with the remaining quartered eggs and parsley and serve immediately with a pinch of cayenne pepper.

2

3

4

# Bouillabaisse

## INGREDIENTS

### Serves 4–6

675 g/1½ lb assorted fish, e.g.
  whiting, mackerel, red mullet,
  salmon and king prawns, cleaned
  and skinned
few saffron strands
3 tbsp olive oil
2 onions, peeled and sliced
2 celery sticks, trimmed and sliced
225 g/8 oz ripe tomatoes, peeled and
  chopped
1 fresh bay leaf
2–3 garlic cloves, peeled and crushed
1 bouquet garni
sea salt and freshly ground black
  pepper
French bread, to serve

1 Cut the fish into thick pieces, peel the prawns, if necessary, and rinse well. Place the saffron strands in a small bowl, cover with warm water and leave to infuse for at least 10 minutes.

2 Heat the oil in a large, heavy-based saucepan or casserole, add the onions and celery and sauté for 5 minutes, stirring occasionally. Add the tomatoes, bay leaf, garlic and bouquet garni and stir until lightly coated with the oil.

3 Transfer to the cooking dish and place the firm fish on the base. Pour in the saffron-infused water and enough water to just cover. Cover with the lid and switch to high. Cook for 1 hour.

4 Add the soft-flesh fish and switch the slow cooker to auto and cook for 2 hours, or reduce the cooker to low and cook for 4 hours. Season to taste with salt and pepper, remove and discard the bouquet garni and serve with French bread.

## FOOD FACT

Bouillabaisse is one of France's most famous dishes. It originated in the city of Marseille in Provence.

2

2

3

# Garlic Baked Monkfish

## INGREDIENTS

### Serves 4

300 g/10 oz parsnips, peeled

350 g/12 oz sweet potatoes, peeled

300 g/10 oz carrots, peeled

2 onions, peeled

4–6 garlic cloves, peeled

salt and freshly ground
  black pepper

450 ml/³/₄ pint hot fish or vegetable
  stock

2 tbsp olive oil

2 small monkfish tails, about
  900 g/ 2 lb total weight, or
  4 monkfish fillets, about
  700 g/1¹/₂ lb total weight

2–3 sprigs fresh rosemary

2 yellow peppers, deseeded

225 g/8 oz cherry tomatoes

2 tbsp freshly chopped parsley

1 Cut all the root vegetables, including the onions, into even-sized wedges and place in the cooking dish. Reserve 2 garlic cloves and add the remainder to the vegetables. Season to taste with salt and pepper and pour over 1 tablespoon of the oil. Turn the vegetables over until lightly coated in the oil. Pour in the stock then cover with the lid and switch the cooker to auto. Cook for 4–5 hours.

2 Meanwhile, cut the monkfish tails into fillets. Using a sharp knife, cut down both sides of the central bone to form 2 fillets from each tail. Discard any skin or membrane, then rinse thoroughly. Make small incisions down the length of the monkfish fillets.

3 Cut the reserved garlic cloves into small slivers and break the rosemary into small sprigs. Insert the garlic and rosemary into the incisions in the fish.

4 Cut the peppers into strips, then add to the vegetables together with the cherry tomatoes. Cook for a further 1 hour. Place the fish on top and drizzle with the remaining oil. Cook for a further 1 hour, or reduce the heat to low and cook for 2 hours or until the vegetables and fish are thoroughly cooked. Serve sprinkled with chopped parsley.

## FOOD FACT

Monkfish is a great fish for slow cooking. It has a very firm, almost meaty texture that allows the fish to stay intact in the pot.

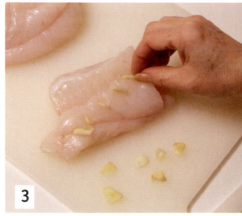

# Aromatic Seafood Curry

## INGREDIENTS

### Serves 4–6

few saffron strands

450 g/1 lb assorted seafood, such as
 prawns, mussels, squid, scallops
 and white fish fillets

2 tbsp groundnut oil

4 green cardamom pods, cracked

2 whole star anise

3 garlic cloves, peeled and crushed

1 bird's eye chilli, deseeded and
 chopped

2 lemon grass stalks, bruised and
 outer leaves discarded

5 cm/2 inch piece fresh root ginger,
 peeled and grated

1–2 tbsp curry paste, or
 to taste

300 ml/½ pint coconut milk

150 ml/¼ pint water

1 tbsp rice wine

4 spring onions, trimmed and
 shredded

freshly cooked Thai fragrant rice,
 to serve

1 Cover the saffron strands in cooled boiled water and leave to soak for at least 10 minutes.

2 Prepare the seafood, cleaning the prawns and discarding the thin black vein, if necessary. Scrub the mussels, discarding any that do not close. Rinse the squid and cut into strips, remove the vein from the scallops and cut in half, if large. Cut the fish fillets into small strips. Reserve.

3 Heat the oil in a large saucepan, add the cardamom pods, star anise, garlic, chilli, lemon grass and ginger and gently fry for 1 minute. Stir in the curry paste and cook for 2 minutes.

4 Take off the heat and gradually stir in the coconut milk and water. Transfer to the cooking dish and cover with the lid. Switch to high and cook for 30 minutes.

5 Add the seafood, starting with the fish pieces, switch the cooker to low and cook for 40 minutes. Stir in the prawns, mussels and scallops and cook for a further 20 minutes. Add the squid with the rice wine and cook for 10 minutes, or until all the fish is tender. Spoon into a warmed serving dish, sprinkle with the spring onions and serve with fragrant rice.

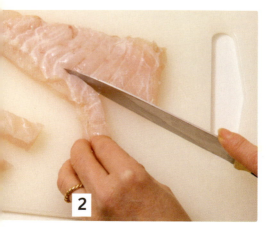

2

3

5

# Spicy Lamb in Yogurt Sauce

## INGREDIENTS

### Serves 4

1 tsp hot chilli powder

1 tsp ground cinnamon

1 tsp medium hot curry powder

1 tsp ground cumin

salt and freshly ground black pepper

2 tbsp groundnut oil

450 g/1 lb lamb fillet, trimmed

4 cardamom pods, bruised

4 whole cloves

1 onion, peeled and finely sliced

2 garlic cloves, peeled and crushed

2.5 cm/1 inch piece fresh root ginger,
   peeled and grated

150 ml/¼ pint Greek-style yogurt

1 tbsp freshly chopped coriander

2 spring onions, trimmed and
   finely sliced

### To serve:

freshly cooked rice

naan bread

### TASTY TIP

Marinating the lamb in this recipe really adds flavour, and also helps tenderise it, even before cooking.

1 Blend the chilli powder, cinnamon, curry powder, cumin and seasoning with 2 tablespoons of the oil in a bowl and reserve.

2 Cut the lamb fillet into thin strips, add to the spice and oil mixture and stir until coated thoroughly. Cover and leave to marinate in the refrigerator for at least 30 minutes.

3 Heat a wok, then pour in the remaining oil. When hot, add the cardamom pods and cloves and stir-fry for 10 seconds. Add the onion, garlic and ginger to the wok and stir-fry for 3–4 minutes until softened. Place the lamb with the marinade into the wok. Then transfer all the ingredients to the cooking dish and cover with the lid.

4 Switch the cooker to auto and cook for 1 hour. Reduce the heat to low. Pour in the yogurt, stir thoroughly and cook for 4–5 hours. Sprinkle with the chopped coriander and sliced spring onions, then serve immediately with freshly cooked rice and naan bread.

# Braised Lamb with Broad Beans

## INGREDIENTS

### Serves 4

700 g/1½ lb lean lamb, cut
   into large chunks
1 tbsp plain flour
1 onion
2 garlic cloves
1 tbsp olive oil
400 g can chopped tomatoes
   with basil
300 ml/½ pint lamb stock
2 tsp dried thyme
2 tsp dried oregano
salt and freshly ground black pepper
150 g/5 oz frozen broad beans,
   thawed
fresh oregano, to garnish
creamy mashed potatoes, to serve

1 Trim the lamb, discarding any fat or gristle, then place the flour in a polythene bag, add the lamb and toss until coated thoroughly. Peel and slice the onion and garlic and reserve.

2 Heat the olive oil in a heavy-based saucepan and, when hot, add the lamb and cook, stirring until the meat is sealed and browned all over. Using a slotted spoon, remove and reserve.

3 Add the onion and garlic to the saucepan and cook for 3 minutes, stirring frequently, until softened, then return the lamb to the saucepan. Add the chopped tomatoes with their juice, the stock, the chopped thyme and oregano to the pan and season to taste with salt and pepper. Bring to the boil, then transfer to the cooking dish. Cover with the lid and switch to low. Cook for 4–6 hours.

4 Add the broad beans to the lamb and continue to cook on low for 2 hours, or until the lamb is tender. Garnish with fresh oregano and serve with creamy mashed potatoes.

## HELPFUL HINT

When adding softer vegetables, such as broad beans, to a slow cooker, you need to add them towards the end of the cooking time or they will become soft and mushy.

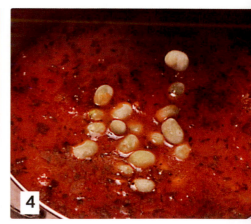

# Spanish-style Pork Stew with Saffron Rice

## INGREDIENTS

### Serves 4

2 tbsp olive oil

900 g/2 lb boneless pork shoulder, diced

1 large onion, peeled and sliced

2 garlic cloves, peeled and finely chopped

1 tbsp plain flour

450 g/1 lb plum tomatoes, peeled and chopped

175 ml/6 fl oz red wine

1 tbsp freshly chopped basil

1 green pepper, deseeded and sliced

50 g/2 oz pimiento-stuffed olives, cut in half crossways

salt and freshly ground black pepper

fresh basil leaves, to garnish

### For the saffron rice:

1 tbsp olive oil

25 g/1 oz butter

1 small onion, peeled and finely chopped

few strands saffron, crushed

250 g/9 oz easy-cook white long-grain rice

600ml/1 pint chicken stock

1   Heat the oil in a flameproof pan or frying pan and fry the pork in batches over a high heat, transferring the cubes to a plate as they brown.

2   Lower the heat and add the onion to the pan. Cook for a further 5 minutes until soft and starting to brown. Add the garlic and stir briefly before returning the pork to the onions. Add the flour and stir.

3   Add the tomatoes. Gradually stir in the red wine and add the basil. Bring to simmering point and carefully transfer to the cooking dish. Cover with the lid and switch the slow cooker to auto. Cook for 1 hour. Stir in the green pepper and olives, then switch to low and cook for 5 hours. Season to taste with salt and pepper.

4   Meanwhile, to make the saffron rice, heat the oil with the butter in a saucepan. Add the onion and cook for 5 minutes over a medium heat until softened. Add the saffron and rice and stir well. Add the stock, bring to the boil, cover and reduce the heat as low as possible. Cook for 15 minutes, covered, until the rice is tender and the stock is absorbed. Adjust the seasoning and serve with the stew, garnished with fresh basil.

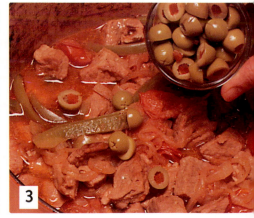

# Pork Goulash & Rice

## INGREDIENTS

### Serves 4

700 g/1½ lb boneless pork chops or
   pork fillet
1 tbsp olive oil
2 onions, peeled and roughly
   chopped
1 red pepper, deseeded and thinly
   sliced
1 garlic clove, peeled and crushed
1 tbsp plain flour
1 rounded tbsp paprika
400 g can chopped tomatoes
salt and freshly ground
   black pepper
250 g/9 oz easy-cook white long-
   grain rice
600 ml/1 pint chicken stock
sprigs of fresh flat-leaf parsley,
   to garnish
150 ml/¼ pint soured cream,
   to serve

## FOOD FACT

Goulash is a classic pork dish that originated in Hungary. It is also popular in Austria, Germany, across Eastern Europe and even in some regions of Italy.

1 Cut the pork into large cubes, about 4 cm/1½ inches square. Heat the oil in a large flameproof dish or frying pan and brown the pork in batches over a high heat, transferring the cubes to a plate as they brown.

2 Over a medium heat, add the onions and pepper and cook for about 5 minutes, stirring regularly, until they begin to brown. Add the garlic and return the meat to the dish or frying pan along with any juices on the plate. Sprinkle in the flour and paprika and stir well to soak up the oil and juices. Add the tomatoes and season to taste with salt and pepper. Bring to the boil, then carefully transfer to the cooking dish. Cover with the lid and switch the cooker to auto. Cook for 2 hours, then reduce the heat to low and cook for 5–6 hours.

3 Just before serving, rinse the rice in several changes of water until the water remains relatively clear. Drain well and put into a saucepan with the chicken stock or water and a little salt. Cover tightly and bring to the boil. Turn the heat down as low as possible and cook for 10 minutes without removing the lid. After 10 minutes, remove from the heat and leave for a further 10 minutes, without removing the lid. Fluff with a fork.

4 When the meat is tender, stir in the soured cream lightly to create a marbled effect, or serve separately. Garnish with parsley and serve immediately with the rice.

# Pork Chop Hotpot

## INGREDIENTS

### Serves 4

4 pork chops
flour, to dust
225 g/8 oz shallots, peeled
2 garlic cloves, peeled
50 g/2 oz sun-dried tomatoes
2 tbsp olive oil
400 g can plum tomatoes
150 ml/¼ pint red wine
150 ml/¼ pint chicken stock
3 tbsp tomato purée
2 tbsp freshly chopped oregano
salt and freshly ground
  black pepper
fresh oregano leaves, to garnish

### To serve:
freshly cooked new potatoes
French beans

## TASTY TIP
When using red wine to cook it is always a good idea to use wine that you would be happy to drink. If you use old wine, for example, it will affect the taste of your dish.

1 Trim the pork chops, removing any excess fat, wipe with a clean, damp cloth, then dust with a little flour and reserve. Cut the shallots in half if large. Chop the garlic and slice the sun-dried tomatoes.

2 Heat the olive oil in a large frying pan and cook the pork chops for about 5 minutes, turning occasionally during cooking, until browned all over. Using a slotted spoon, carefully lift out of the pan and reserve. Add the shallots and cook for 5 minutes, stirring occasionally.

3 Place the pork chops in the cooking dish and scatter with the garlic and sun-dried tomatoes, then pour over the can of tomatoes with their juice.

4 Blend the red wine, stock and tomato purée together and add the chopped oregano. Season to taste with salt and pepper, then pour over the pork chops. Cover with the lid and switch the slow cooker to auto. Cook for 5–7 hours, or until the pork chops are tender. Adjust the seasoning to taste, then scatter with a few oregano leaves and serve immediately with freshly cooked potatoes and French beans.

# Italian Beef 'Pot Roast'

## INGREDIENTS

## Serves 6

1.8 kg/4 lb brisket of beef
225 g/8 oz small onions, peeled
3 garlic cloves, peeled and chopped
2 celery sticks, trimmed
  and chopped
2 carrots, peeled and sliced
450 g/1 lb ripe tomatoes
300 ml/½ pint Italian red wine
2 tbsp olive oil
300 ml/½ pint beef stock
1 tbsp tomato purée
2 tsp freeze-dried
  mixed herbs
salt and freshly ground
  black pepper
25 g/1 oz butter
25 g/1 oz plain flour
freshly cooked vegetables, to serve

1   Place the beef in a bowl. Add the onions, garlic, celery and carrots. Place the tomatoes in a separate small bowl and cover with boiling water. Allow to stand for 2 minutes and drain. Peel away the skins, discard the seeds and chop, then add to the bowl with the red wine. Cover tightly and marinate in the refrigerator overnight.

2   Lift the marinated beef from the bowl and pat dry with absorbent kitchen paper. Heat the olive oil in a large frying pan and cook the beef until it is browned all over, then remove and place in the cooking dish. Drain the vegetables, reserving the marinade. Add the vegetables to the frying pan and fry gently for 5 minutes, stirring occasionally, until all the vegetables are browned. Place in the cooking dish.

3   Blend the marinade, beef stock, tomato purée, mixed herbs and seasoning together. Bring to the boil, then pour over the beef and cover with the lid. Switch the slow cooker to auto and cook for 3 hours, then switch to low and cook for 8–10 hours.

4   Using a slotted spoon, transfer the beef and any large vegetables to a plate and leave in a warm place. Blend the butter and flour to form a paste. Pour the meat juices into a small saucepan and bring to the boil. Gradually stir in small spoonfuls of the butter and flour paste. Cook until thickened. Serve the beef with the sauce and a selection of freshly cooked vegetables.

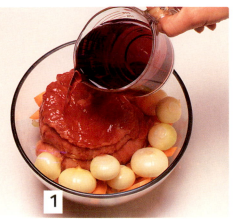

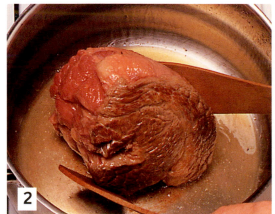

# Beef Bourguignon

## INGREDIENTS

### Serves 4

675 g/1½ lb braising steak, trimmed

225 g/8 oz piece pork belly or lardons

2 tbsp olive oil

12 shallots, peeled

2 garlic cloves, peeled
  and sliced

225 g/8 oz carrots, peeled and sliced

2 tbsp plain flour

3 tbsp brandy (optional)

150 ml/¼ pint red wine, such as
  a Burgundy

450 ml/¾ pint beef stock

1 bay leaf

salt and freshly ground
  black pepper

450 g/1 lb new potatoes, scrubbed

1 tbsp freshly chopped parsley,
  to garnish

## FOOD FACT

Beef Bourguignon is 'the' classic French dish. It originated in Burgundy, in eastern France, and the wine used to cook it is also typically from that region. It is sometimes served with pasta.

1 Cut the steak and pork into small pieces and reserve. Heat 1 tablespoon of the oil in a frying pan, add the meat and cook in batches for 5–8 minutes, or until sealed. Remove with a slotted spoon and reserve.

2 Add the remaining oil to the pan, then add the shallots, carrots and garlic and cook for 10 minutes. Return the meat to the shallots and sprinkle in the flour. Cook for 2 minutes, stirring occasionally, before pouring in the brandy. Heat for 1 minute, then take off the heat and ignite.

3 When the flames have subsided, pour in the wine and stock. Return to the heat and bring to the boil, stirring constantly.

4 Transfer to the cooking dish. Cut the potatoes in half and stir into the meat. Add the bay leaf and season to taste with salt and pepper. Cover with the lid and switch the slow cooker to high. Cook for 2 hours.

5 Turn the slow cooker to low and continue to cook for 8–10 hours, or until the meat and potatoes are tender. Serve sprinkled with chopped parsley.

1

2

3

# Steak & Kidney Stew

## INGREDIENTS

### Serves 4

1 tbsp olive oil

1 onion, peeled and chopped

2–3 garlic cloves, peeled and crushed

2 celery sticks, trimmed and sliced

550 g/1¼ lb braising steak, trimmed and diced

125 g/4 oz lambs' kidneys, cored and chopped

2 tbsp plain flour

1 tbsp tomato purée

900 ml/1½ pints beef stock

salt and freshly ground black pepper

1 fresh bay leaf

300 g/10 oz carrots, peeled and sliced

350 g/12 oz baby new potatoes, scrubbed

350 g/12 oz fresh spinach leaves, chopped

### For the dumplings:

125 g/4 oz self-raising flour

50 g/2 oz shredded suet

1 tbsp freshly chopped mixed herbs

2–3 tbsp water

1 Heat the oil in a large, heavy-based saucepan, add the onion, garlic and celery and sauté for 5 minutes, or until browned. Remove from the pan with a slotted spoon and reserve.

2 Add the steak and kidneys to the pan and cook for 3–5 minutes, or until sealed, then return the onion mixture to the pan. Sprinkle in the flour and cook, stirring, for 2 minutes. Take off the heat, stir in the tomato purée, then the stock, and season to taste with salt and pepper. Add the bay leaf.

3 Return to the heat and bring to the boil, stirring occasionally. Add the carrots and potatoes, then carefully transfer to the cooking dish. Cover with the lid and switch the slow cooker to high. Cook for 1 hour, then switch to low and cook for 6–8 hours.

4 Place the flour, suet and herbs in a bowl and add a little seasoning. Add the water and mix to a stiff mixture. Using a little extra flour, shape into 8 small balls. Place the dumplings on top of the stew and cover with the lid. Return the slow cooker to high and cook for 30 minutes–1 hour. Switch the cooker off and stir in the spinach. Leave to stand for 2 minutes, or until the spinach is wilted.

1

4

4

# Braised Chicken in Beer

## INGREDIENTS

### Serves 4

4 chicken joints, skinned
125 g/4 oz pitted dried prunes
2 bay leaves
12 shallots
2 tsp olive oil
125 g/4 oz small button mushrooms,
   wiped
1 tsp soft dark brown sugar
½ tsp whole-grain mustard
2 tsp tomato purée
150 ml/¼ pint light ale
150 ml/¼ pint chicken stock
salt and freshly ground
   black pepper
2 tsp cornflour
2 tsp lemon juice
2 tbsp chopped fresh parsley
flat-leaf parsley, to garnish

### To serve:
mashed potatoes
seasonal green vegetables

1 Cut each chicken joint in half and put in the cooking dish together with the prunes and bay leaves.

2 To peel the shallots, put in a small bowl and cover with boiling water. Drain the shallots after 2 minutes and rinse under cold water until cool enough to handle. The skins should then peel away easily from the shallots.

3 Heat the oil in a large, heavy-based frying pan. Add the shallots and cook gently for about 5 minutes until beginning to colour. Add the mushrooms to the pan and cook for a further 3–4 minutes until both the mushrooms and onions are softened. Sprinkle the sugar over the shallots and mushrooms, then add the mustard, tomato purée, ale and chicken stock. Season to taste with salt and pepper and bring to the boil, stirring to blend. Carefully pour over the chicken.

4 Cover the cooking dish with the lid and switch the slow cooker to high. Cook for 3 hours. Blend the cornflour with the lemon juice and 1 tablespoon of cold water and stir into the chicken and cook on high for a further 1 hour, or until the chicken is tender. Remove the bay leaves and stir in the chopped parsley. Serve with the mashed potatoes and fresh green vegetables. Garnish the chicken with the flat-leaf parsley.

# Chicken & White Wine Risotto

## INGREDIENTS

### Serves 4–6

2 tbsp oil

125 g/4 oz unsalted butter

2 shallots, peeled and finely chopped

300 g/11 oz easy-cook or Arborio rice

300 ml/1½ pint dry white wine

750 ml/1¼ pints chicken stock,
  heated

350 g/12 oz skinless chicken breast
  fillets, thinly sliced

50 g/2 oz Parmesan cheese, grated

2 tbsp freshly chopped dill or parsley

salt and freshly ground black pepper

1 Heat half the oil and half the butter in a large, heavy-based saucepan over a medium-high heat. Add the shallots and cook for 2 minutes, or until softened, stirring frequently. Add the rice and cook for 2–3 minutes, stirring frequently, until the rice is translucent and well coated.

2 Pour in the wine and 150 ml/¼ pint of the stock, then bring to the boil. It will bubble and steam rapidly. When it has subsided, transfer to the cooking dish. Wipe the pan clean and heat the remaining oil. Add the chicken to the saucepan and cook for 5 minutes, or until sealed, turning the chicken over at least once.

3 Add the chicken to the cooking dish together with most of the stock. Cover with the lid. Switch the slow cooker to high and cook for 2 hours. Stir once during cooking, adding the remaining stock if it is becoming dry.

4 Switch the slow cooker to auto and stir in the remaining butter with the Parmesan cheese, half the chopped herbs and seasoning to taste. Cook for 30 minutes. Switch the cooker off and leave to stand for 10 minutes. Spoon into warmed shallow bowls and sprinkle each with the remaining chopped herbs. Serve immediately.

## HANDY HINT

Risotto is a tricky dish to get right. You should taste the rice towards the end of the cooking time; it should be cooked but still firm to bite. Overcooked risotto will start to become stodgy.

# Chicken Gumbo

## INGREDIENTS

## Serves 4

8 small skinless chicken portions

1 tbsp olive oil

15 g/½ oz unsalted butter

1 onion, peeled and chopped

2–3 garlic cloves, peeled and chopped

1–2 red chillies, deseeded and chopped

2 celery sticks, trimmed and sliced

1 red pepper, deseeded and chopped

225 g/8 oz okra, trimmed and sliced

4 spicy sausages

2 tbsp plain flour

1.7 litres/3 pints chicken stock

few dashes of Tabasco sauce

6 spring onions, trimmed and chopped

2 x 250 g/9 oz packets pre-cooked basmati rice, to serve

## FOOD FACT

Okra are the seed pods of the okra plant, and are used in dishes around the world, from India to the Far East, to the Caribbean. When added to a dish, their juices will thicken the sauce.

1 Rinse the chicken portions and pat dry on absorbent kitchen paper. Heat the oil and butter in a large, heavy-based saucepan, add the chicken and fry, in batches, for 8–10 minutes, or until lightly browned. Remove with a slotted spoon or metal tongs and reserve.

2 Add all the vegetables to the pan and fry for 8 minutes, or until the vegetables are beginning to soften. Remove with a slotted spoon and reserve.

3 Add the sausages to the pan and cook for 5–8 minutes, or until browned all over, then remove and cut each sausage in half. Add half the browned vegetables to the pan and sprinkle in the flour. Cook for 2 minutes, then gradually stir in the stock. Bring to the boil, then transfer to the cooking dish together with the chicken and sausages. Cover with the lid and switch the slow cooker to high. Cook for 3 hours.

4 Add the remaining vegetables together with a few dashes of Tabasco. Re-cover with the lid and cook on high for 30 minutes. Stir in the spring onions.

5 Heat the rice according to the packet instructions, then place a serving in a deep bowl. Ladle a portion of the gumbo over the rice and serve.

1

2

3

# Chicken Cacciatore

## INGREDIENTS

### Serves 4

2–3 tbsp olive oil

125 g/4 oz pancetta or streaky bacon,
  diced

1.4 kg/3 lb chicken, cut into
  8 pieces

25 g/1 oz plain flour

salt and freshly ground
  black pepper

2 garlic cloves, peeled and chopped

125 ml/4 fl oz red wine

400 g can chopped tomatoes

150 ml/¼ pint chicken stock

12 small onions, peeled

1 bay leaf

1 tsp brown sugar

1 tsp dried oregano

1 green pepper, deseeded and
  chopped

225 g/8 oz chestnut or field
  mushrooms, thickly sliced

2 tbsp freshly chopped parsley

freshly cooked tagliatelle, to serve

1 Heat 1 tablespoon of the olive oil in a large deep frying pan and add the diced pancetta or bacon and fry for 2–3 minutes, or until crisp and golden brown. Using a slotted spoon, transfer the pancetta or bacon to the cooking dish.

2 Lightly rinse the chicken and dry on absorbent kitchen paper. Season the flour with salt and pepper, then use to coat the chicken. Heat the remaining oil in the pan and brown the chicken pieces on all sides for about 15 minutes. Remove from the pan and add to the cooking dish.

3 Stir the garlic into the pan and cook for about 30 seconds. Add the red wine and cook, stirring and scraping any browned bits from the base of the pan. Allow the wine to boil until it is reduced by half. Add the tomatoes, stock, onions, bay leaf, brown sugar and oregano and stir well. Season to taste.

4 Bring the tomato mixture to the boil, then pour over the chicken. Cover with the lid and switch the slow cooker to high. Cook for 2 hours. Stir in the peppers and mushrooms, re-cover and cook for a further 1 hour, or until the chicken and vegetables are tender. Stir in the chopped parsley and serve immediately with freshly cooked tagliatelle.

2

3

4

# Chicken Marengo

## INGREDIENTS

### Serves 4

2 tbsp plain flour

salt and freshly ground black pepper

4 boneless, skinless chicken breasts,
  cut into bite-size pieces

4 tbsp olive oil

1 Spanish onion, peeled
  and chopped

1 garlic clove, peeled and chopped

400 g can chopped tomatoes

2 tbsp tomato purée

3 tbsp freshly chopped basil

3 tbsp freshly chopped thyme

125 ml/4 fl oz dry white wine or
  chicken stock

350 g/12 oz rigatoni

3 tbsp freshly chopped flat-leaf
  parsley

1 Season the flour with salt and pepper and toss the chicken in the flour to coat. Heat 2 tablespoons of the olive oil in a large frying pan and cook the chicken for 5–7 minutes, or until browned all over, turning occasionally. Remove from the pan using a slotted spoon and reserve.

2 Add the remaining oil to the pan, add the onion and cook, stirring occasionally, for 5 minutes, or until softened and starting to brown. Add the garlic, tomatoes, tomato purée, basil and thyme. Pour in the wine or chicken stock and season to taste. Bring to the boil, then reintroduce the chicken. Then transfer to the cooking dish. Cover with the lid and switch the slow cooker to high. Cook for 3–4 hours, or until the chicken is thoroughly cooked.

3 Just before serving, bring a large pan of lightly salted water to a rolling boil. Add the rigatoni and cook according to the packet instructions, or until al dente.

4 Drain the rigatoni thoroughly, return to the pan and stir in the chopped parsley. Tip the pasta into a warmed large serving dish or spoon on to individual plates. Spoon over the chicken with the sauce and serve immediately.

## FOOD FACT

Chicken Marengo is a French savoury dish. Apparently, it takes its name from being the dish that Napoléon Bonaparte ate after the Battle of Marengo in 1800.

1

2

4

# Chicken Chasseur

## INGREDIENTS

### Serves 4

1 whole chicken, about 1.4 kg/3 lb in
  weight, jointed into 4 or 8 portions
1 tbsp olive oil
15 g/¹/₂ oz unsalted butter
12 baby onions, peeled
2–4 garlic cloves, peeled
  and sliced
2 celery sticks, trimmed and sliced
175 g/6 oz closed cup mushrooms,
  wiped
2 tbsp plain flour
300 ml/¹/₂ pint dry white wine
2 tbsp tomato purée
450 ml/³/₄ pint chicken stock
salt and freshly ground
  black pepper
1 tsp dried tarragon or few sprigs
  of fresh tarragon
350 g/12 oz sweet potatoes, peeled
  and cut into chunks
300 g/10 oz shelled fresh or frozen
  broad beans
1 tbsp freshly chopped tarragon,
  to garnish

1 Skin the chicken, if preferred, and rinse lightly. Pat dry on absorbent kitchen paper. Heat the oil and butter in a heavy-based frying pan, add the chicken portions and fry for 5–8 minutes, in batches, until browned all over. Remove with a slotted spoon and place in the cooking dish.

2 Add the onions, garlic and celery to the frying pan and cook for 5 minutes, or until golden. Cut the mushrooms in half if large, then add to the pan and cook for 2 minutes.

3 Sprinkle in the flour and cook for 2 minutes, then gradually stir in the wine. Blend the tomato purée with a little of the stock in a small bowl, then stir into the pan together with the remaining stock, seasoning to taste, and the dried or fresh tarragon. Bring to the boil, stirring constantly.

4 Pour the sauce over the chicken and cover with the lid. Switch the slow cooker to high and cook for 3 hours.

5 Stir in the sweet potatoes. Re-cover with the lid and continue to cook for a further 30 minutes. Add the broad beans and cook for a further 30 minutes, or until the chicken and vegetables are cooked. Serve sprinkled with freshly chopped tarragon.

1

2

3

# Thai-flavoured Chicken

## INGREDIENTS

### Serves 4–6

1 tsp cumin seeds

1 tsp mustard seeds

1 tsp coriander seeds

1 tsp turmeric

1 bird's eye chilli, deseeded and
   finely chopped

1 tbsp freshly grated root ginger

2 garlic cloves, peeled and finely
   chopped

125 ml/4 fl oz double cream

8 skinless chicken thighs

2 tbsp groundnut oil

1 onion, peeled and finely sliced

200 ml/7 fl oz chicken stock

salt and freshly ground
   black pepper

4 tbsp freshly chopped coriander

2 spring onions, shredded,
   to garnish

freshly cooked Thai fragrant rice,
   to serve

1 Heat a wok or heavy-based frying pan and add the cumin seeds, mustard seeds and coriander seeds. Dry-fry over a low to medium heat for 2 minutes, or until the fragrance becomes stronger and the seeds start to pop. Add the turmeric and leave to cool. Grind the spices in a pestle and mortar or blend to a fine powder in a food processor.

2 Mix the chilli, ginger, garlic and the cream together in a small bowl, add the ground spices and mix. Place the chicken thighs in a shallow dish and spread the spice paste over the thighs.

3 Heat the wok or frying pan and add the oil and, when hot, add the onion and fry until golden brown. Add the chicken and spice paste. Cook for 5–6 minutes, stirring occasionally, until evenly coloured. Add the stock and season to taste with salt and pepper.

4 Transfer to the cooking dish. Cover with the lid and switch the slow cooker to high. Cook for 3–4 hours, or until the chicken is thoroughly cooked. Stir in the chopped coriander and serve immediately with the freshly cooked rice sprinkled with shredded spring onions.

1

2

3

# Light Ratatouille

## INGREDIENTS

## Serves 4

1 red pepper

2 courgettes, trimmed

1 small aubergine, trimmed

1 onion, peeled

2 ripe tomatoes

50 g/2 oz button mushrooms, wiped
  and halved or quartered

200 ml/7 fl oz tomato juice

1 tbsp freshly chopped basil

salt and freshly ground black pepper

1. Deseed the peppers, remove the membrane with a small sharp knife and cut into small dice. Thickly slice the courgettes and cut the aubergine into small cubes. Slice the onion into rings.

2. Place the tomatoes in boiling water until their skins begin to peel away.

3. Remove the skins from the tomatoes, cut into quarters and remove the seeds.

4. Place all the vegetables in the cooking dish with the tomato juice and basil. Season to taste with salt and pepper.

5. Cover with the lid and switch the slow cooker to auto. Cook for 1½ hours, or until tender but still retain a bite, al dente.

6. Remove the vegetables with a slotted spoon and arrange in a serving dish.

7. Pour the liquid into a saucepan and bring to the boil. Boil for 20 seconds until it is slightly thickened. Season the sauce to taste with salt and pepper.

8. Pass the sauce through a sieve to remove some of the seeds and pour over the vegetables. Serve the ratatouille hot or cold.

## TASTY TIP

Ratatouille is a lovely dish eaten hot. It actually tastes even better served cold the next day, after the flavours have become more infused with the vegetables.

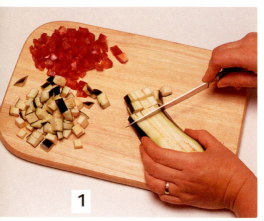

1

4

6

# Vegetable & Lentil Casserole

## INGREDIENTS

### Serves 4

225 g/8 oz Puy lentils

1–2 tbsp olive oil

1 onion, peeled and chopped

2–3 garlic cloves, peeled and crushed

300 g/10 oz carrots, peeled and
   sliced into chunks

3 celery sticks, trimmed and sliced

350 g/12 oz butternut squash, peeled,
   seeds removed and diced

1 litre/1¾ pints vegetable stock

salt and freshly ground black pepper

few sprigs fresh oregano, plus extra
   to garnish

1 large red pepper, deseeded and
   chopped

2 courgettes, trimmed and sliced

150 ml/¼ pint soured cream,
   to serve

1 Pour the lentils out on to a plate and look through them for any small stones, then rinse the lentils and reserve.

2 Heat the oil in a deep frying pan, add the onion, garlic, carrots and celery and sauté for 5 minutes, stirring occasionally.

3 Add the squash and lentils. Pour in the stock and season to taste with salt and pepper. Add the oregano sprigs and bring to the boil.

4 Carefully transfer to the cooking dish and cover with the lid. Switch the slow cooker to low and cook for 6 hours.

5 Add the red pepper and courgettes and stir. Continue to cook for a further 1–2 hours, or until all the vegetables are tender. Adjust the seasoning, garnish with sprigs of fresh oregano and serve with soured cream.

## HANDY HINT

If you are on a budget, lentils are a great way to add protein to vegetarian meals. They are much cheaper than meat, whether you buy them dried or in cans.

1

2

3

# Vegetable & Coconut Pot

## INGREDIENTS

### Serves 4–6

2 tbsp vegetable oil or ghee

1 tsp cumin seeds

1 cinnamon stick, bruised

3 whole cloves

3 cardamom pods, bruised

½–1 tsp chilli powder

8 shallots, peeled and halved

2–3 garlic cloves, peeled and finely chopped

225 g/8 oz potatoes, peeled and cut into chunks

½ butternut squash, about 350 g/12 oz in weight, peeled, deseeded and cut into chunks

225 g/8 oz carrots, peeled and chopped

200 ml/7 fl oz water

300 ml/½ pint coconut milk

225 g/8 oz French beans, trimmed and chopped

400 g/14 oz can red kidney beans, drained and rinsed

4–6 spring onions, trimmed and finely chopped

1. Heat the oil or ghee in a large saucepan, add the seeds, cinnamon stick, cloves, cardamom pods and chilli powder and fry for 30 seconds, or until the seeds pop.

2. Add the shallots, garlic, potatoes, squash and carrots and stir until the vegetables are coated in the flavoured oil. Add the water, bring to the boil, then carefully transfer to the cooking dish. Cover with the lid.

3. Switch the slow cooker to low and cook for 6 hours. Pour in the coconut milk and add the chopped beans and kidney beans, stir gently until thoroughly mixed together.

4. Continue to cook for a further 2 hours, or until the vegetables are tender. Sprinkle with the chopped spring onions and serve.

1

2

3

# Step-by-Step, Practical Recipes Slow Cooker: Tips & Hints

## Helpful Hint

There are many different types of slow cooker, in all styles and colours, from rustic earthenware to shiny stainless steel. Originally they were only available as a round pot, but these days they also come in an oval shape, which is ideal for cooking small whole fish and joints of meat such as a pot roast. All cookers have a ceramic or toughened glass lid and many are now detachable from their cooking base so they can also be used on the hob or in the oven as though they were a conventional pot. You should always carefully read the manufacturer's booklet before you use your slow cooker.

## Tasty Tip

If you are marinating meat, before you cook it in a slow cooker, it is always a good idea to give the marinating process as much time as possible. With Beef Bourguignon (see p24), if you have the time, increase the amount of wine to around half a bottle and marinate the beef in the refrigerator overnight.

## Helpful Hint

For some foods you need to factor in the longer cooking time and lower temperature of a slow cooker. Root vegetables, for example, should be cut into small pieces and covered in liquid. Squashes, pumpkins and courgettes are quicker to cook than root vegetables and so should be added at the end of the cooking time. Poultry should be cooked on high to ensure that any bacteria are destroyed, while dried beans and pulses should be soaked and cooked beforehand, as though you were using them normally. Sugar and dairy products do not respond well to slow cooking; if a recipe calls for cream add it at the end. Use dried herbs rather than fresh as they retain their flavour better over the longer cooking time.

## Helpful Hint

If you are looking for a really good quality cut of meat for some of the slow cooker recipes in this book, then it sometimes pays to go to a good butcher, rather than just to the supermarket. They will trim the meat professionally so there is not too much waste, and they should also be able to order any unusual cuts of meat for you.

## Tasty Tip

Many of the recipes in this book use some or a lot of garlic. It is a very, very versatile ingredient. A good tip, for when you want a weaker garlic taste, is to leave the garlic clove unpeeled. For a bit more strength, crush the unpeeled clove and for a really robust flavour peel the garlic fully before adding to your dish.

## Food Fact

Paprika is the ground red powder of the dried pepper *Capsicum annum* and is a vital ingredient for dishes such as Pork Goulash (see p18). It gives a really distinctive colour and taste to most meals. It is very popular in Central European cooking and in Moroccan cuisine where it is made into a paste by the addition of some olive oil. It is also sometimes added to henna to give a reddish tint to hair!

## Tasty Tip

As well as using wine for cooking, there are lots of other ways to use alcoholic drinks to enhance the flavour of your slow-cooked meals. Beer, used for example in Braised Chicken in Beer (see p28), is used in stews all over Europe. From Beef in Beer in the north of England to the famous Carbonnade à la Flamande from Belgium, a thick stew of beer, bacon, onions, and brown sugar.

## Tasty Tip

Bouillabaisse (see p6) was traditionally eaten as a communal meal, and used up to eight different types of fresh fish and seafood. To make this, and any other fish dish, particularly tasty, try to make your own fish stock to add to the dish when cooking. You can do this by putting small pieces of the fish skeleton into a pan of water with chopped onion, carrot and celery, and a bay leaf, and simmer for about 20 minutes. Do not used the fish heads that usually come attached to the skeleton, as the gills will make the stock bitter, and do not use the bones of oily fish as they are usually a little too rich and smelly.

---

First published in 2012 by
**FLAME TREE PUBLISHING LTD**
Crabtree Hall, Crabtree Lane, Fulham,
London, SW6 6TY, United Kingdom
www.flametreepublishing.com

The CIP record for this book is available from the British Library • Printed in China

NOTE: Recipes using uncooked eggs should be avoided by infants, the elderly, pregnant women and anyone suffering from an illness.

18 17 16 15 14 13 12   10 9 8 7 6 5 4 3 2 1

ISBN: 978-0-85775-608-4

ACKNOWLEDGEMENTS: Authors: Catherine Atkinson, Juliet Barker, Gina Steer, Vicki Smallwood, Carol Tennant, Mari Mererid Williams, Elizabeth Wolf-Cohen and Simone Wright. Photography: Colin Bowling, Paul Forrester and Stephen Brayne. Home Economists and Stylists: Jacqueline Bellefontaine, Mandy Phipps, Vicki Smallwood and Penny Stephens. All props supplied by Barbara Stewart at Surfaces. Publisher and Creative Director: Nick Wells. Editorial: Catherine Taylor, Sarah Goulding, Marcus Hardie, Gina Steer and Karen Fitzpatrick. Design and Production: Chris Herbert, Mike Spender, Colin Rudderham and Helen Wall.